This Planner Belongs To:

____

Grown Woman
Life Financial Goal Planner
Unapologetically Wisdom Line
A Division of The Dream Ink House

Typeset & Editing by: Dream Loud Ink Publishing
Email : info@thedreaminkhouse.com or dreamloudinc@yahoo.com

INTRODUCTION

The goal for this financial plan book is to help us be more intentional about our finances. It does not matter if you have personal debt, student loans or a lack of savings. We all have to start somewhere and begin taking responsibility in our financial matters. If you are waiting for someone to come and sprinkle fairy dust, or possibly win the lottery, you are wasting your time. This financial guide is in no way a form of advice. I am not a licensed financial advisor, nor do I hold any certifications in this area. I am on a personal debt-free journey to financial freedom and building a savings security because I believe that is the key to fulfilling dreams, and to becoming successful in business endeavors. This guide is designed to help you see your vision on paper so that you can take guided action steps towards completing them. On the following page, there is an interactive breakdown on how to use this planner and summaries of each template. There is also a pre-planning section before the first month to help you set yourself up for success. Much success to you and your journey on knocking out your financial goals and becoming the best financial version of yourself.

The *Unapologetically Wisdom Line* was created to purpose an impact of prayer, growth, wisdom and financial stability over specific areas of our lives, while being intentional on our personal journey's to becoming better stewards over what God has positioned us with.

Toi Nichelle

12 Month
HOW TO USE THIS PLANNER

YOU CAN START PLANNING ANY MONTH OF THE YEAR

PRE-PLANNING

CONTENTS	HOW TO USE
A YEAR IN A GLANCE	VI USE THIS SECTION TO MAP OUT YOUR MAIN FINANCIAL GOALS FOR THE YEAR YOU WISH TO ACCOMPLISH.
FINANCIAL PURPOSE	VII USE THIS SECTION TO LIST WHAT YOUR FINANCIAL STATUS LOOKS LIKE NOW VS. WHAT YOUR FUTURE FINANCIAL GOALS ARE.
FINANCIAL PRIORITIES	VIII USE THIS SECTION TO LIST YOUR FINANCIAL PRIORITIES FOR THE YEAR SO THAT YOU CAN REMAIN FOCUSED.
5 YEAR FINANCIAL PLAN	IX-X USE THIS SECTION TO MAP OUT WHERE YOU SEE YOURSELF IN THE NEXT FIVE YEARS.
PLANNING FOR LIFE'S FINANCIAL CURVEBALLS	XI USE THIS SECTION TO DO AN INVENTORY OF YOUR IDENTITY, SECURE IMPORTANT DOCUMENTS AND CONSIDER INSURANCE OPTIONS.
IMPORTANT PHONE NUMBERS	XII USE THIS SECTION TO LIST IMPORTANT NUMBERS YOU NEED TO KEEP TRACK OF REGARDING YOUR FINANCES.
YEARLY EXPENSES	XIII USE THIS SECTION TO LIST YOUR ONE-TIME YEARLY EXPENSES FOR THE YEAR AND DETERMINE YOUR NEEDS VS. WANTS.

PRE – PLANNING

CONTENTS	HOW TO USE
YEARLY TAX REFUND	XIV USE THIS SECTION TO MAP OUT YOUR MAIN FINANCIAL GOALS FOR THE YEAR YOU WISH TO ACCOMPLISH.
ANNUAL CREDIT REPORT	XV USE THIS SPACE TO JOT DOWN YOUR CREDIT REPORTS AND THE THREE DEBTS YOU WISH TO TACKLE THIS YEAR
CREDIT DISPUTE / CLEAN UP	XVI USE THIS SECTION TO KEEP TRACK OF THE CREDIT ITEMS YOU WISH TO DISPUTE AND/OR GET REMOVED
STUDENT LOAN DEBT PAYMENTS	XVII-XVIII USE THIS SECTION TO KEEP TRACK OF STUDENT LOAN PAYMENTS
SAVINGS GOAL	XIX USE THIS SECTION TO MAP OUT YOUR SAVINGS GOAL FOR THE YEAR
IMPORTANT PASSWORDS	XX USE THIS SECTION TO KEEP TRACK OF ANY PASSWORDS FOR ONLINE BILLS, INSURANCE, BANKING ETC.

MONTHLY - PLANNING

CONTENTS

HOW TO USE

CONTENTS

HOW TO USE

A Year in a Glance

USE THIS SECTION TO LIST ANY YEARLY BILLS,
STREAMS OF INCOME OR FINANCIAL GOALS

JANUARY	FEBRUARY	MARCH
APRIL	MAY	JUNE
JULY	AUGUST	SEPTEMBER
OCTOBER	NOVEMBER	DECEMBER

What's My Financial Purpose?

WHAT DOES MY FINANCIAL FUTURE LOOK LIKE?

WHAT IS MY OVERALL FINANCIAL PURPOSE IN LIFE?

What Are My Financial Priorities?

FINANCIAL WORDS FOR THE YEAR

My Why

MY TOP 3 FINANCIAL PRIORITIES

1. ______________________________

2. ______________________________

3. ______________________________

My 5 Year Financial Plan

USE THIS SECTION TO BRIEFLY JOT DOWN YOUR LIFE'S VISION

Short Notes

WHERE DO I SEE MYSELF FINANCIALLY I
N FIVE YEARS?

WHAT DOES IT LOOK LIKE?

PURCHASE A HOME?

SAVINGS/DEBT?

FAMILY?

TRAVEL/VACATIONS?

Short Notes

Planning For Life's Financial Curveballs

IDENTITY MONITORING (WHAT METHODS I USE?)

____

____

____

HOW CAN I BETTER MONITOR MY IDENTITY?

____

____

____

DO I HAVE PERSONAL LIFE INSURANCE? IF NOT, WHY? IF YES, HOW'S IT WORKING FOR ME? IS IT AFFORDABLE FOR MY FAMILY?

____

____

____

ARE THESE ITEMS IN A SECURE PLACE? AVAILABLE COPIES?

- ☐ BIRTH CERTIFICATE
- ☐ SOCIAL SECURITY CARD
- ☐ PASSPORT
- ☐ EXTRA EMERGENCY CASH

Short Notes

Important Phone Numbers

USE THIS SPACE TO LIST IMPORTANT FINANCIAL NUMBERS

AGENCY	CONTACT
FREE CREDIT REPORT	
COLLECTION AGENCY	

BANK	
HUMAN RESOURCES (WORK)	
RETIREMENT ACCOUNT	
LIFE INSURANCE	
IDENTITY THEFT	
UNEMPLOYMENT	
SOCIAL SECURITY	

My Yearly Expenses

USE THIS SPACE TO JOT DOWN ANY YEARLY (ONCE A YEAR) BILLS

PAYEE	AMOUNT	DATE

TOTAL: $ ____________________

Short Notes

My Yearly Tax Refund

USE THIS SPACE TO JOT DOWN HOW YOU PLAN TO USE YOUR REFUND

DATE TO FILE

ITEMS NEEDED TO FILE: ______________________

- ☐ ______________________ ☐ ______________________
- ☐ ______________________ ☐ ______________________
- ☐ ______________________ ☐ ______________________

EXPECTED REFUND: ______________________

ACTUAL REFUND: ______________________

HOW MUCH TO SAVINGS: ______________________

HOW MUCH TO DEBT? ______________________

MULTIPLE STREAMS OF INCOME? LIST THEM HERE.

My Annual Credit Report

USE THIS SPACE TO JOT DOWN YOUR CREDIT REPORTS AND THE THREE DEBTS YOU WISH TO TACKLE THIS YEAR

REQUEST YOUR REPORTS FOR FREE AT WWW.ANNUALCREDITREPORT.COM

DATE: DATE:

EXPERIAN

REQUESTED? ________ RECEIVED? ________ SCORE? ________

EQUIFAX

REQUESTED? ________ RECEIVED? ________ SCORE? ________

TRANSUNION

REQUESTED? ________ RECEIVED? ________ SCORE? ________

WHAT ARE THREE SMALLEST ITEMS ON YOUR CREDIT THAT NEEDS TO BE ADDRESSED?

1. ________________________________

2. ________________________________

3. ________________________________

Credit Dispute / Clean Up

USE THIS SECTION TO KEEP TRACK OF THE CREDIT ITEMS
YOU WISH TO DISPUTE AND/OR GET REMOVED

ITEM DESCRIPTION	CREDIT CONTACT	FOLLOW-UP DATE	OUTCOME

Short Notes

Student Loan Debt Payments

USE THIS SECTION TO KEEP TRACK OF STUDENT LOAN PAYMENTS

BEGINNING DEBT AMOUNT	PAYMENT AMOUNT	DATE

Student Loan Debt Payments

CONTINUED...

BEGINNING DEBT AMOUNT	PAYMENT AMOUNT	DATE

Savings Goal

HOW MUCH WOULD YOU LIKE TO SAVE THIS YEAR?

$ ______________________

MONTH	AMOUNT	DATE

END OF YEAR AMOUNT: $ ______________________

Important Passwords

USE THIS SECTION TO KEEP TRACK OF ANY PASSWORDS FOR ONLINE BILLS, INSURANCE, BANKING ETC.

BUSINESS / AGENCY	PASSWORD

Short Notes

Month 1

Monthly Expense Tracker

USE THIS SECTION TO KEEP TRACK OF MONTHLY EXPENSES
OUTSIDE OF YOUR BUDGET. WAS THE ITEM A NEED OR A WANT?

ITEM DESCRIPTION	AMOUNT SPENT	NEED / WANT?

TOTAL: ______________________

Paycheck Budget #1

USE THIS SECTION TO KEEP TRACK OF MONTHLY EXPENSES.
IF YOU HAVE MORE BILLS THAN THE SPACE LISTED, REEVALUATE WHAT'S IMPORTANT.

MONTH OF: ______________________

PAYCHECK #1 GROSS INCOME: ______________________

NEXT PAYCHECK: ______________

TAXES/DEDUCTIONS TAKEN OUT: ______________________

PAYCHECK #1 NET INCOME: ______________________

ANY FINANCIAL EMERGENCIES
HAPPEN THIS MONTH?
LIST THEM BELOW.

PAYEE	AMOUNT	DATE	BALANCE

BILL TOTAL: ______________

Bi-Weekly Financial To Do List

USE THIS SECTION TO LIST ANY TASKS OR ERRANDS NEEDED FOR THE WEEK.
FOR EXAMPLE, MAKING A BANK WITHDRAWAL OR DEPOSITING MONEY IN SAVINGS.

WEEK 1: ____________________

FINANCIAL GOAL
1. ____________________
2. ____________________
3. ____________________

WEEK 2: ____________________

FINANCIAL GOAL
1. ____________________
2. ____________________
3. ____________________

Paycheck Budget #2

USE THIS SECTION TO KEEP TRACK OF MONTHLY EXPENSES.
IF YOU HAVE MORE BILLS THAN THE SPACE LISTED, REEVALUATE WHAT'S IMPORTANT.

MONTH OF: ____________________

NEXT PAYCHECK: ______________

PAYCHECK #1 GROSS INCOME: ____________________

TAXES/DEDUCTIONS TAKEN OUT: ________________

PAYCHECK #1 NET INCOME: ____________________

ANY FINANCIAL EMERGENCIES
HAPPEN THIS MONTH?
LIST THEM BELOW.

PAYEE	AMOUNT	DATE	BALANCE

BILL TOTAL: ______________

Bi-Weekly Financial To Do List

USE THIS SECTION TO LIST ANY TASKS OR ERRANDS NEEDED FOR THE WEEK.
FOR EXAMPLE, MAKING A BANK WITHDRAWAL OR DEPOSITING MONEY IN SAVINGS.

WEEK 3: ____________

FINANCIAL GOAL
1. ____________
2. ____________
3. ____________

WEEK 4: ____________

FINANCIAL GOAL
1. ____________
2. ____________
3. ____________

My Monthly Savings Plan

USE THIS SECTION TO LIST YOUR SAVINGS GOAL
AND MONTHLY CONTRIBUTIONS

IF AN UNEXPECTED EMERGENCY HAPPENED, HOW MUCH WOULD I NEED TO SURVIVE FOR 6 MONTHS?

$____________________

ONE YEAR? $____________________

HOW MUCH SAVINGS WOULD MAKE ME FEEL "SAFE"? $____________________

CURRENT MONTHLY SAVINGS CONTRIBUTION $____________________

CUSHION SAVINGS GOAL? $____________________

SEPARATE RETIREMENT ACCOUNTS (MONTHLY) $____________________

CAN I INCREASE MY CONTRIBUTION THIS MONTH? $____________________

IF YES, BY HOW MUCH? $____________________

RETIREMENT (WORK-RELATED)? $____________________

IRA ROTH? $____________________

IRA TRADITIONAL? $____________________

ANY UNEXPECTED MONEY THIS MONTH?

IF YES, HOW WILL I USE IT? ______________________________

____

____

My Monthly Debt Payoff

USE THIS SECTION TO LIST ALL YOUR DEBTS YOU ARE CURRENTLY PAYING ON EACH MONTH

PAYEE	CURRENT BALANCE	AMOUNT PAID	ENDING BALANCE	DATE

Y
O
U

G
O
T

T
H
I
S

TOTAL DEBT BEFORE PAYMENTS: $ ____________________

TOTAL AMOUNT AFTER PAYMENTS $ ____________________

Monthly Notes

Month 2

Monthly Expense Tracker

USE THIS SECTION TO KEEP TRACK OF MONTHLY EXPENSES
OUTSIDE OF YOUR BUDGET. WAS THE ITEM A NEED OR A WANT?

ITEM DESCRIPTION	AMOUNT SPENT	NEED / WANT?

TOTAL: ____________________

Paycheck Budget #1

USE THIS SECTION TO KEEP TRACK OF MONTHLY EXPENSES.
IF YOU HAVE MORE BILLS THAN THE SPACE LISTED, REEVALUATE WHAT'S IMPORTANT.

MONTH OF: ____________________

PAYCHECK #1 GROSS INCOME: ____________________

NEXT PAYCHECK: ______________

TAXES/DEDUCTIONS TAKEN OUT: ________________

PAYCHECK #1 NET INCOME: ____________________

ANY FINANCIAL EMERGENCIES
HAPPEN THIS MONTH?
LIST THEM BELOW.

PAYEE	AMOUNT	DATE	BALANCE

BILL TOTAL: ______________

Bi-Weekly Financial To Do List

USE THIS SECTION TO LIST ANY TASKS OR ERRANDS NEEDED FOR THE WEEK.
FOR EXAMPLE, MAKING A BANK WITHDRAWAL OR DEPOSITING MONEY IN SAVINGS.

WEEK 1: ________________

FINANCIAL GOAL
1. ________________
2. ________________
3. ________________

WEEK 2: ________________

FINANCIAL GOAL
1. ________________
2. ________________
3. ________________

Paycheck Budget #2

USE THIS SECTION TO KEEP TRACK OF MONTHLY EXPENSES.
IF YOU HAVE MORE BILLS THAN THE SPACE LISTED, REEVALUATE WHAT'S IMPORTANT.

MONTH OF: ____________________

PAYCHECK #1 GROSS INCOME: ____________________

NEXT PAYCHECK: ______________

TAXES/DEDUCTIONS TAKEN OUT: ________________

PAYCHECK #1 NET INCOME: ____________________

ANY FINANCIAL EMERGENCIES
HAPPEN THIS MONTH?
LIST THEM BELOW.

PAYEE	AMOUNT	DATE	BALANCE

BILL TOTAL: ______________

Bi-Weekly Financial To Do List

USE THIS SECTION TO LIST ANY TASKS OR ERRANDS NEEDED FOR THE WEEK.
FOR EXAMPLE, MAKING A BANK WITHDRAWAL OR DEPOSITING MONEY IN SAVINGS.

WEEK 3: ____________________

FINANCIAL GOAL
1. ______________________________
2. ______________________________
3. ______________________________

WEEK 4: ____________________

FINANCIAL GOAL
1. ______________________________
2. ______________________________
3. ______________________________

My Monthly Savings Plan

USE THIS SECTION TO LIST YOUR SAVINGS GOAL
AND MONTHLY CONTRIBUTIONS

IF AN UNEXPECTED EMERGENCY HAPPENED, HOW MUCH WOULD I NEED TO SURVIVE FOR 6 MONTHS?

$______________________

ONE YEAR? $______________________

HOW MUCH SAVINGS WOULD MAKE ME FEEL "SAFE"? $______________________

CURRENT MONTHLY SAVINGS CONTRIBUTION $______________________

CUSHION SAVINGS GOAL? $______________________

SEPARATE RETIREMENT ACCOUNTS (MONTHLY) $______________________

CAN I INCREASE MY CONTRIBUTION THIS MONTH? $______________________

IF YES, BY HOW MUCH? $______________________

RETIREMENT (WORK-RELATED)? $______________________

IRA ROTH? $______________________

IRA TRADITIONAL? $______________________

ANY UNEXPECTED MONEY THIS MONTH?

IF YES, HOW WILL I USE IT? ______________________________________

____

____

My Monthly Debt Payoff

USE THIS SECTION TO LIST ALL YOUR DEBTS YOU ARE CURRENTLY PAYING ON EACH MONTH

Y O U G O T T H I S

PAYEE	CURRENT BALANCE	AMOUNT PAID	ENDING BALANCE	DATE

TOTAL DEBT BEFORE PAYMENTS: $ ______________________

TOTAL AMOUNT AFTER PAYMENTS $ ______________________

Monthly Notes

Month 3

Monthly Expense Tracker

USE THIS SECTION TO KEEP TRACK OF MONTHLY EXPENSES
OUTSIDE OF YOUR BUDGET. WAS THE ITEM A NEED OR A WANT?

ITEM DESCRIPTION	AMOUNT SPENT	NEED / WANT?

TOTAL: ____________________

Paycheck Budget #1

USE THIS SECTION TO KEEP TRACK OF MONTHLY EXPENSES.
IF YOU HAVE MORE BILLS THAN THE SPACE LISTED, REEVALUATE WHAT'S IMPORTANT.

MONTH OF: ____________________

PAYCHECK #1 GROSS INCOME: ____________________

NEXT PAYCHECK: ______________

TAXES/DEDUCTIONS TAKEN OUT: ____________________

PAYCHECK #1 NET INCOME: ____________________

PAYEE	AMOUNT	DATE	BALANCE

ANY FINANCIAL EMERGENCIES HAPPEN THIS MONTH? LIST THEM BELOW.

____
____
____
____

____
____
____
____

BILL TOTAL: ______________

Bi-Weekly Financial To Do List

USE THIS SECTION TO LIST ANY TASKS OR ERRANDS NEEDED FOR THE WEEK.
FOR EXAMPLE, MAKING A BANK WITHDRAWAL OR DEPOSITING MONEY IN SAVINGS.

WEEK 1: ____________________

FINANCIAL GOAL
1. ______________________________
2. ______________________________
3. ______________________________

WEEK 2: ____________________

FINANCIAL GOAL
1. ______________________________
2. ______________________________
3. ______________________________

Paycheck Budget #2

USE THIS SECTION TO KEEP TRACK OF MONTHLY EXPENSES.
IF YOU HAVE MORE BILLS THAN THE SPACE LISTED, REEVALUATE WHAT'S IMPORTANT.

MONTH OF: ______________________

NEXT PAYCHECK: ______________

PAYCHECK #1 GROSS INCOME: ____________________

TAXES/DEDUCTIONS TAKEN OUT: __________________

PAYCHECK #1 NET INCOME: ______________________

ANY FINANCIAL EMERGENCIES
HAPPEN THIS MONTH?
LIST THEM BELOW.

PAYEE	AMOUNT	DATE	BALANCE

BILL TOTAL: ______________

Bi-Weekly Financial To Do List

USE THIS SECTION TO LIST ANY TASKS OR ERRANDS NEEDED FOR THE WEEK.
FOR EXAMPLE, MAKING A BANK WITHDRAWAL OR DEPOSITING MONEY IN SAVINGS.

WEEK 3: ______________

FINANCIAL GOAL
1. ________________________
2. ________________________
3. ________________________

WEEK 4: ______________

FINANCIAL GOAL
1. ________________________
2. ________________________
3. ________________________

My Monthly Savings Plan

USE THIS SECTION TO LIST YOUR SAVINGS GOAL
AND MONTHLY CONTRIBUTIONS

IF AN UNEXPECTED EMERGENCY HAPPENED, HOW MUCH WOULD I NEED TO SURVIVE FOR 6 MONTHS?

$______________________

ONE YEAR? $______________________

HOW MUCH SAVINGS WOULD MAKE ME FEEL "SAFE"? $______________________

CURRENT MONTHLY SAVINGS CONTRIBUTION $______________________

CUSHION SAVINGS GOAL? $______________________

SEPARATE RETIREMENT ACCOUNTS (MONTHLY) $______________________

CAN I INCREASE MY CONTRIBUTION THIS MONTH? $______________________

IF YES, BY HOW MUCH? $______________________

RETIREMENT (WORK-RELATED)? $______________________

IRA ROTH? $______________________

IRA TRADITIONAL? $______________________

ANY UNEXPECTED MONEY THIS MONTH?

IF YES, HOW WILL I USE IT?

____

____

____

My Monthly Debt Payoff

USE THIS SECTION TO LIST ALL YOUR DEBTS YOU ARE CURRENTLY PAYING ON EACH MONTH

YOU GOT THIS

PAYEE	CURRENT BALANCE	AMOUNT PAID	ENDING BALANCE	DATE

TOTAL DEBT BEFORE PAYMENTS: $ ______________________

TOTAL AMOUNT AFTER PAYMENTS $ ______________________

Monthly Notes

1st Quarter Check-In

My Financial Check-in

USE THIS SECTION TO TAKE ACCOUNTABILITY AND BE HONEST
WITH YOUR JOURNEY OVER THE PAST THREE MONTHS.

REVIEW

HOW'S IT GOING SO FAR? ANY SETBACKS? ANY MILESTONES?

ADJUST

WHAT CAN I DO TO ADJUST THIS SETBACK? HOW WILL I CELEBRATE THIS MILESTONE?

Short Notes

Financial Check-in Continued...

EXECUTE

HOW WILL I IMPLEMENT THIS NEW ADJUSTMENT INTO MY FINANCIAL PLAN?

MONITOR

WHAT DOES MY FINANCIAL MONITORING ROUTINE LOOK LIKE? IS IT WORKING?

Short Notes

Credit Score Check-In

HAVE YOU CHECKED YOUR CREDIT?

AVAILABLE ONLINE RESOURCES:

CREDIT KARMA
WWW.CREDITKARMA.COM

CREDIT SESAME
WWW.CREDITSESAME.COM

EXPERIAN
WWW.EXPERIAN.COM

EQUIFAX
WWW.EQUIFAX.COM

TRANSUNION
WWW.TRANSUNION.COM

MY FICO SCORE
WWW.MYFICO.COM

EXPERIAN SCORE

EQUIFAX SCORE

Short Notes

TRANSUNIION SCORE

LIST YOUR GOAL SCORE HERE:

WHAT ARE SOME THINGS I CAN DO TO INCREASE MY CREDIT IN THE NEXT QUARTER?

Month 4

Monthly Expense Tracker

USE THIS SECTION TO KEEP TRACK OF MONTHLY EXPENSES
OUTSIDE OF YOUR BUDGET. WAS THE ITEM A NEED OR A WANT?

ITEM DESCRIPTION	AMOUNT SPENT	NEED / WANT?

TOTAL: ____________________

Paycheck Budget #1

USE THIS SECTION TO KEEP TRACK OF MONTHLY EXPENSES.
IF YOU HAVE MORE BILLS THAN THE SPACE LISTED, REEVALUATE WHAT'S IMPORTANT.

MONTH OF: ______________________

PAYCHECK #1 GROSS INCOME: ______________________

NEXT PAYCHECK: ______________

TAXES/DEDUCTIONS TAKEN OUT: ______________________

PAYCHECK #1 NET INCOME: ______________________

ANY FINANCIAL EMERGENCIES HAPPEN THIS MONTH? LIST THEM BELOW.

____

____

____

____

____

____

____

____

PAYEE	AMOUNT	DATE	BALANCE

BILL TOTAL: ______________

Bi-Weekly Financial To Do List

USE THIS SECTION TO LIST ANY TASKS OR ERRANDS NEEDED FOR THE WEEK.
FOR EXAMPLE, MAKING A BANK WITHDRAWAL OR DEPOSITING MONEY IN SAVINGS.

WEEK 1: ____________________

FINANCIAL GOAL
1. ______________________________
2. ______________________________
3. ______________________________

WEEK 2: ____________________

FINANCIAL GOAL
1. ______________________________
2. ______________________________
3. ______________________________

Paycheck Budget #2

USE THIS SECTION TO KEEP TRACK OF MONTHLY EXPENSES.
IF YOU HAVE MORE BILLS THAN THE SPACE LISTED, REEVALUATE WHAT'S IMPORTANT.

MONTH OF: ____________________

PAYCHECK #1 GROSS INCOME: ____________________

NEXT PAYCHECK: ______________

TAXES/DEDUCTIONS TAKEN OUT: ________________

PAYCHECK #1 NET INCOME: ____________________

ANY FINANCIAL EMERGENCIES
HAPPEN THIS MONTH?
LIST THEM BELOW.

PAYEE	AMOUNT	DATE	BALANCE

BILL TOTAL: ______________

Bi-Weekly Financial To Do List

USE THIS SECTION TO LIST ANY TASKS OR ERRANDS NEEDED FOR THE WEEK.
FOR EXAMPLE, MAKING A BANK WITHDRAWAL OR DEPOSITING MONEY IN SAVINGS.

WEEK 3: ________________

FINANCIAL GOAL
1. ________________
2. ________________
3. ________________

WEEK 4: ________________

FINANCIAL GOAL
1. ________________
2. ________________
3. ________________

My Monthly Savings Plan

USE THIS SECTION TO LIST YOUR SAVINGS GOAL
AND MONTHLY CONTRIBUTIONS

IF AN UNEXPECTED EMERGENCY HAPPENED, HOW MUCH WOULD I NEED TO SURVIVE FOR 6 MONTHS?

$____________________

ONE YEAR? $____________________

HOW MUCH SAVINGS WOULD MAKE ME FEEL "SAFE"? $____________________

CURRENT MONTHLY SAVINGS CONTRIBUTION $____________________

CUSHION SAVINGS GOAL? $____________________

SEPARATE RETIREMENT ACCOUNTS (MONTHLY) $____________________

CAN I INCREASE MY CONTRIBUTION THIS MONTH? $____________________

IF YES, BY HOW MUCH? $____________________

RETIREMENT (WORK-RELATED)? $____________________

IRA ROTH? $____________________

IRA TRADITIONAL? $____________________

ANY UNEXPECTED MONEY THIS MONTH?

IF YES, HOW WILL I USE IT? ____________________________________

____

____

My Monthly Debt Payoff

USE THIS SECTION TO LIST ALL YOUR DEBTS YOU ARE CURRENTLY PAYING ON EACH MONTH

PAYEE	CURRENT BALANCE	AMOUNT PAID	ENDING BALANCE	DATE

YOU GOT THIS

TOTAL DEBT BEFORE PAYMENTS: $ ______________________

TOTAL AMOUNT AFTER PAYMENTS $ ______________________

Monthly Notes

Month 5

Monthly Expense Tracker

USE THIS SECTION TO KEEP TRACK OF MONTHLY EXPENSES OUTSIDE OF YOUR BUDGET. WAS THE ITEM A NEED OR A WANT?

ITEM DESCRIPTION	AMOUNT SPENT	NEED / WANT?

TOTAL: ____________________

Paycheck Budget #1

USE THIS SECTION TO KEEP TRACK OF MONTHLY EXPENSES.
IF YOU HAVE MORE BILLS THAN THE SPACE LISTED, REEVALUATE WHAT'S IMPORTANT.

MONTH OF: ____________________

PAYCHECK #1 GROSS INCOME: ____________________

NEXT PAYCHECK: ____________________

TAXES/DEDUCTIONS TAKEN OUT: ____________________

PAYCHECK #1 NET INCOME: ____________________

PAYEE	AMOUNT	DATE	BALANCE

ANY FINANCIAL EMERGENCIES
HAPPEN THIS MONTH?
LIST THEM BELOW.

____

____

____

____

____

____

____

____

BILL TOTAL: ____________________

Bi-Weekly Financial To Do List

USE THIS SECTION TO LIST ANY TASKS OR ERRANDS NEEDED FOR THE WEEK.
FOR EXAMPLE, MAKING A BANK WITHDRAWAL OR DEPOSITING MONEY IN SAVINGS.

WEEK 1: ____________________

FINANCIAL GOAL
1. ____________________
2. ____________________
3. ____________________

WEEK 2: ____________________

FINANCIAL GOAL
1. ____________________
2. ____________________
3. ____________________

Paycheck Budget #2

USE THIS SECTION TO KEEP TRACK OF MONTHLY EXPENSES.
IF YOU HAVE MORE BILLS THAN THE SPACE LISTED, REEVALUATE WHAT'S IMPORTANT.

MONTH OF: ______________________

PAYCHECK #1 GROSS INCOME: ______________________

NEXT PAYCHECK: ______________

TAXES/DEDUCTIONS TAKEN OUT: ______________________

PAYCHECK #1 NET INCOME: ______________________

ANY FINANCIAL EMERGENCIES HAPPEN THIS MONTH? LIST THEM BELOW.

PAYEE	AMOUNT	DATE	BALANCE

BILL TOTAL: ______________

Bi-Weekly Financial To Do List

USE THIS SECTION TO LIST ANY TASKS OR ERRANDS NEEDED FOR THE WEEK.
FOR EXAMPLE, MAKING A BANK WITHDRAWAL OR DEPOSITING MONEY IN SAVINGS.

WEEK 3: ____________________

FINANCIAL GOAL
1. ______________________________
2. ______________________________
3. ______________________________

WEEK 4: ____________________

FINANCIAL GOAL
1. ______________________________
2. ______________________________
3. ______________________________

My Monthly Savings Plan

USE THIS SECTION TO LIST YOUR SAVINGS GOAL
AND MONTHLY CONTRIBUTIONS

IF AN UNEXPECTED EMERGENCY HAPPENED, HOW MUCH WOULD
I NEED TO SURVIVE FOR 6 MONTHS?

$______________________

ONE YEAR? $______________________

HOW MUCH SAVINGS WOULD MAKE ME FEEL "SAFE"? $______________________

CURRENT MONTHLY SAVINGS CONTRIBUTION $______________________

CUSHION SAVINGS GOAL? $______________________

SEPARATE RETIREMENT ACCOUNTS (MONTHLY) $______________________

CAN I INCREASE MY CONTRIBUTION THIS MONTH? $______________________

IF YES, BY HOW MUCH? $______________________

RETIREMENT (WORK-RELATED)? $______________________

IRA ROTH? $______________________

IRA TRADITIONAL? $______________________

ANY UNEXPECTED MONEY THIS MONTH?

IF YES, HOW WILL I USE IT? ______________________________________

____

____

My Monthly Debt Payoff

USE THIS SECTION TO LIST ALL YOUR DEBTS YOU ARE CURRENTLY PAYING ON EACH MONTH

PAYEE	CURRENT BALANCE	AMOUNT PAID	ENDING BALANCE	DATE

YOU GOT THIS

TOTAL DEBT BEFORE PAYMENTS: $ ______________________

TOTAL AMOUNT AFTER PAYMENTS $ ______________________

Monthly Notes

Month 6

Monthly Expense Tracker

USE THIS SECTION TO KEEP TRACK OF MONTHLY EXPENSES OUTSIDE OF YOUR BUDGET. WAS THE ITEM A NEED OR A WANT?

ITEM DESCRIPTION	AMOUNT SPENT	NEED / WANT?

TOTAL: ____________________

Paycheck Budget #1

USE THIS SECTION TO KEEP TRACK OF MONTHLY EXPENSES.
IF YOU HAVE MORE BILLS THAN THE SPACE LISTED, REEVALUATE WHAT'S IMPORTANT.

MONTH OF: ______________________

PAYCHECK #1 GROSS INCOME: ____________________

NEXT PAYCHECK: ______________

TAXES/DEDUCTIONS TAKEN OUT: __________________

PAYCHECK #1 NET INCOME: ______________________

ANY FINANCIAL EMERGENCIES
HAPPEN THIS MONTH?
LIST THEM BELOW.

PAYEE	AMOUNT	DATE	BALANCE

BILL TOTAL: ______________

Bi-Weekly Financial To Do List

USE THIS SECTION TO LIST ANY TASKS OR ERRANDS NEEDED FOR THE WEEK.
FOR EXAMPLE, MAKING A BANK WITHDRAWAL OR DEPOSITING MONEY IN SAVINGS.

WEEK 1: ________________

FINANCIAL GOAL
1. ______________________________
2. ______________________________
3. ______________________________

WEEK 2: ________________

FINANCIAL GOAL
1. ______________________________
2. ______________________________
3. ______________________________

Paycheck Budget #2

USE THIS SECTION TO KEEP TRACK OF MONTHLY EXPENSES.
IF YOU HAVE MORE BILLS THAN THE SPACE LISTED, REEVALUATE WHAT'S IMPORTANT.

MONTH OF: ______________________

PAYCHECK #1 GROSS INCOME: ____________________

NEXT PAYCHECK: ______________

TAXES/DEDUCTIONS TAKEN OUT: __________________

PAYCHECK #1 NET INCOME: ______________________

ANY FINANCIAL EMERGENCIES
HAPPEN THIS MONTH?
LIST THEM BELOW.

PAYEE	AMOUNT	DATE	BALANCE

____

____

____

____

____

____

____

____

BILL TOTAL: ______________

Bi-Weekly Financial To Do List

USE THIS SECTION TO LIST ANY TASKS OR ERRANDS NEEDED FOR THE WEEK.
FOR EXAMPLE, MAKING A BANK WITHDRAWAL OR DEPOSITING MONEY IN SAVINGS.

WEEK 3: ____________________

FINANCIAL GOAL

1. ____________________

2. ____________________

3. ____________________

WEEK 4: ____________________

FINANCIAL GOAL

1. ____________________

2. ____________________

3. ____________________

My Monthly Savings Plan

USE THIS SECTION TO LIST YOUR SAVINGS GOAL
AND MONTHLY CONTRIBUTIONS

IF AN UNEXPECTED EMERGENCY HAPPENED, HOW MUCH WOULD I NEED TO SURVIVE FOR 6 MONTHS?

$______________________

ONE YEAR? $______________________

HOW MUCH SAVINGS WOULD MAKE ME FEEL "SAFE"? $______________________

CURRENT MONTHLY SAVINGS CONTRIBUTION $______________________

CUSHION SAVINGS GOAL? $______________________

SEPARATE RETIREMENT ACCOUNTS (MONTHLY) $______________________

CAN I INCREASE MY CONTRIBUTION THIS MONTH? $______________________

IF YES, BY HOW MUCH? $______________________

RETIREMENT (WORK-RELATED)? $______________________

IRA ROTH? $______________________

IRA TRADITIONAL? $______________________

ANY UNEXPECTED MONEY THIS MONTH?

IF YES, HOW WILL I USE IT? ______________________________________

____

____

My Monthly Debt Payoff

USE THIS SECTION TO LIST ALL YOUR DEBTS YOU ARE CURRENTLY PAYING ON EACH MONTH

PAYEE	CURRENT BALANCE	AMOUNT PAID	ENDING BALANCE	DATE

YOU GOT THIS

TOTAL DEBT BEFORE PAYMENTS: $ ______________________

TOTAL AMOUNT AFTER PAYMENTS $ ______________________

Monthly Notes

2nd Quarter Check-In

My Financial Check-in

USE THIS SECTION TO TAKE ACCOUNTABILITY AND BE HONEST
WITH YOUR JOURNEY OVER THE PAST THREE MONTHS.

REVIEW

HOW'S IT GOING SO FAR? ANY SETBACKS? ANY MILESTONES?

ADJUST

WHAT CAN I DO TO ADJUST THIS SETBACK? HOW WILL I CELEBRATE THIS MILESTONE?

Short Notes

Financial Check-in Continued...

EXECUTE

HOW WILL I IMPLEMENT THIS NEW ADJUSTMENT INTO MY FINANCIAL PLAN?

MONITOR

WHAT DOES MY FINANCIAL MONITORING ROUTINE LOOK LIKE? IS IT WORKING?

Short Notes

Credit Score Check-In

HAVE YOU CHECKED YOUR CREDIT?

AVAILABLE ONLINE RESOURCES:

CREDIT KARMA
WWW.CREDITKARMA.COM

CREDIT SESAME
WWW.CREDITSESAME.COM

EXPERIAN
WWW.EXPERIAN.COM

EQUIFAX
WWW.EQUIFAX.COM

TRANSUNION
WWW.TRANSUNION.COM

MY FICO SCORE
WWW.MYFICO.COM

EXPERIAN SCORE

EQUIFAX SCORE

Short Notes

TRANSUNIION SCORE

LIST YOUR GOAL SCORE HERE:

WHAT ARE SOME THINGS I CAN DO TO INCREASE MY CREDIT IN THE NEXT QUARTER?

Month 7

Monthly Expense Tracker

USE THIS SECTION TO KEEP TRACK OF MONTHLY EXPENSES OUTSIDE OF YOUR BUDGET. WAS THE ITEM A NEED OR A WANT?

ITEM DESCRIPTION	AMOUNT SPENT	NEED / WANT?

TOTAL: ____________________

Paycheck Budget #1

USE THIS SECTION TO KEEP TRACK OF MONTHLY EXPENSES.
IF YOU HAVE MORE BILLS THAN THE SPACE LISTED, REEVALUATE WHAT'S IMPORTANT.

MONTH OF: ____________________

NEXT PAYCHECK: ______________

PAYCHECK #1 GROSS INCOME: ____________________

TAXES/DEDUCTIONS TAKEN OUT: ________________

PAYCHECK #1 NET INCOME: ____________________

ANY FINANCIAL EMERGENCIES HAPPEN THIS MONTH? LIST THEM BELOW.

PAYEE	AMOUNT	DATE	BALANCE

BILL TOTAL: ______________

Bi-Weekly Financial To Do List

USE THIS SECTION TO LIST ANY TASKS OR ERRANDS NEEDED FOR THE WEEK.
FOR EXAMPLE, MAKING A BANK WITHDRAWAL OR DEPOSITING MONEY IN SAVINGS.

WEEK 1: ____________________

FINANCIAL GOAL
1. ______________________________
2. ______________________________
3. ______________________________

WEEK 2: ____________________

FINANCIAL GOAL
1. ______________________________
2. ______________________________
3. ______________________________

Paycheck Budget #2

USE THIS SECTION TO KEEP TRACK OF MONTHLY EXPENSES.
IF YOU HAVE MORE BILLS THAN THE SPACE LISTED, REEVALUATE WHAT'S IMPORTANT.

MONTH OF: ____________________

NEXT PAYCHECK: ____________________

PAYCHECK #1 GROSS INCOME: ____________________

TAXES/DEDUCTIONS TAKEN OUT: ____________________

PAYCHECK #1 NET INCOME: ____________________

ANY FINANCIAL EMERGENCIES HAPPEN THIS MONTH? LIST THEM BELOW.

____
____
____
____
____
____
____
____

PAYEE	AMOUNT	DATE	BALANCE

BILL TOTAL: ____________________

Bi-Weekly Financial To Do List

USE THIS SECTION TO LIST ANY TASKS OR ERRANDS NEEDED FOR THE WEEK.
FOR EXAMPLE, MAKING A BANK WITHDRAWAL OR DEPOSITING MONEY IN SAVINGS.

WEEK 3: ______________

FINANCIAL GOAL
1. ______________
2. ______________
3. ______________

WEEK 4: ______________

FINANCIAL GOAL
1. ______________
2. ______________
3. ______________

My Monthly Savings Plan

USE THIS SECTION TO LIST YOUR SAVINGS GOAL
AND MONTHLY CONTRIBUTIONS

IF AN UNEXPECTED EMERGENCY HAPPENED, HOW MUCH WOULD I NEED TO SURVIVE FOR 6 MONTHS?

$______________________

ONE YEAR? $______________________

HOW MUCH SAVINGS WOULD MAKE ME FEEL "SAFE"? $______________________

CURRENT MONTHLY SAVINGS CONTRIBUTION $______________________

CUSHION SAVINGS GOAL? $______________________

SEPARATE RETIREMENT ACCOUNTS (MONTHLY) $______________________

CAN I INCREASE MY CONTRIBUTION THIS MONTH? $______________________

IF YES, BY HOW MUCH? $______________________

RETIREMENT (WORK-RELATED)? $______________________

IRA ROTH? $______________________

IRA TRADITIONAL? $______________________

ANY UNEXPECTED MONEY THIS MONTH?

IF YES, HOW WILL I USE IT? ______________________

____

____

My Monthly Debt Payoff

USE THIS SECTION TO LIST ALL YOUR DEBTS YOU ARE CURRENTLY PAYING ON EACH MONTH

PAYEE	CURRENT BALANCE	AMOUNT PAID	ENDING BALANCE	DATE

TOTAL DEBT BEFORE PAYMENTS: $ ____________________

TOTAL AMOUNT AFTER PAYMENTS $ ____________________

YOU GOT THIS

Monthly Notes

Month 8

Monthly Expense Tracker

USE THIS SECTION TO KEEP TRACK OF MONTHLY EXPENSES
OUTSIDE OF YOUR BUDGET. WAS THE ITEM A NEED OR A WANT?

ITEM DESCRIPTION	AMOUNT SPENT	NEED / WANT?

TOTAL: ____________________

Paycheck Budget #1

USE THIS SECTION TO KEEP TRACK OF MONTHLY EXPENSES.
IF YOU HAVE MORE BILLS THAN THE SPACE LISTED, REEVALUATE WHAT'S IMPORTANT.

MONTH OF: ______________________

PAYCHECK #1 GROSS INCOME: ____________________

NEXT PAYCHECK: ______________

TAXES/DEDUCTIONS TAKEN OUT: __________________

PAYCHECK #1 NET INCOME: ______________________

ANY FINANCIAL EMERGENCIES
HAPPEN THIS MONTH?
LIST THEM BELOW.

PAYEE	AMOUNT	DATE	BALANCE

BILL TOTAL: ______________

Bi-Weekly Financial To Do List

USE THIS SECTION TO LIST ANY TASKS OR ERRANDS NEEDED FOR THE WEEK.
FOR EXAMPLE, MAKING A BANK WITHDRAWAL OR DEPOSITING MONEY IN SAVINGS.

WEEK 1: ____________________

FINANCIAL GOAL
1. ______________________________
2. ______________________________
3. ______________________________

WEEK 2: ____________________

FINANCIAL GOAL
1. ______________________________
2. ______________________________
3. ______________________________

Paycheck Budget #2

USE THIS SECTION TO KEEP TRACK OF MONTHLY EXPENSES.
IF YOU HAVE MORE BILLS THAN THE SPACE LISTED, REEVALUATE WHAT'S IMPORTANT.

MONTH OF: ____________________

PAYCHECK #1 GROSS INCOME: ____________________

NEXT PAYCHECK: ____________________

TAXES/DEDUCTIONS TAKEN OUT: ____________________

PAYCHECK #1 NET INCOME: ____________________

PAYEE	AMOUNT	DATE	BALANCE

ANY FINANCIAL EMERGENCIES
HAPPEN THIS MONTH?
LIST THEM BELOW.

____

____

____

____

____

____

____

____

BILL TOTAL: ____________________

Bi-Weekly Financial To Do List

USE THIS SECTION TO LIST ANY TASKS OR ERRANDS NEEDED FOR THE WEEK.
FOR EXAMPLE, MAKING A BANK WITHDRAWAL OR DEPOSITING MONEY IN SAVINGS.

WEEK 3: ________________

FINANCIAL GOAL
1. ______________________________
2. ______________________________
3. ______________________________

WEEK 4: ________________

FINANCIAL GOAL
1. ______________________________
2. ______________________________
3. ______________________________

My Monthly Savings Plan

USE THIS SECTION TO LIST YOUR SAVINGS GOAL
AND MONTHLY CONTRIBUTIONS

IF AN UNEXPECTED EMERGENCY HAPPENED, HOW MUCH WOULD I NEED TO SURVIVE FOR 6 MONTHS?

$______________________

ONE YEAR? $______________________

HOW MUCH SAVINGS WOULD MAKE ME FEEL "SAFE"? $______________________

CURRENT MONTHLY SAVINGS CONTRIBUTION $______________________

CUSHION SAVINGS GOAL? $______________________

SEPARATE RETIREMENT ACCOUNTS (MONTHLY) $______________________

CAN I INCREASE MY CONTRIBUTION THIS MONTH? $______________________

IF YES, BY HOW MUCH? $______________________

RETIREMENT (WORK-RELATED)? $______________________

IRA ROTH? $______________________

IRA TRADITIONAL? $______________________

ANY UNEXPECTED MONEY THIS MONTH?

IF YES, HOW WILL I USE IT?

____

____

____

My Monthly Debt Payoff

USE THIS SECTION TO LIST ALL YOUR DEBTS YOU ARE CURRENTLY PAYING ON EACH MONTH

YOU GOT THIS

PAYEE	CURRENT BALANCE	AMOUNT PAID	ENDING BALANCE	DATE

TOTAL DEBT BEFORE PAYMENTS: $ ____________________

TOTAL AMOUNT AFTER PAYMENTS $ ____________________

Monthly Notes

Month 9

Monthly Expense Tracker

USE THIS SECTION TO KEEP TRACK OF MONTHLY EXPENSES
OUTSIDE OF YOUR BUDGET. WAS THE ITEM A NEED OR A WANT?

ITEM DESCRIPTION	AMOUNT SPENT	NEED / WANT?

TOTAL: ____________________

Paycheck Budget #1

USE THIS SECTION TO KEEP TRACK OF MONTHLY EXPENSES.
IF YOU HAVE MORE BILLS THAN THE SPACE LISTED, REEVALUATE WHAT'S IMPORTANT.

MONTH OF: ______________________

NEXT PAYCHECK: ______________

PAYCHECK #1 GROSS INCOME: ____________________

TAXES/DEDUCTIONS TAKEN OUT: __________________

PAYCHECK #1 NET INCOME: ______________________

ANY FINANCIAL EMERGENCIES HAPPEN THIS MONTH? LIST THEM BELOW.

PAYEE	AMOUNT	DATE	BALANCE

BILL TOTAL: ______________

Bi-Weekly Financial To Do List

USE THIS SECTION TO LIST ANY TASKS OR ERRANDS NEEDED FOR THE WEEK.
FOR EXAMPLE, MAKING A BANK WITHDRAWAL OR DEPOSITING MONEY IN SAVINGS.

WEEK 1: ____________________

FINANCIAL GOAL
1. ____________________
2. ____________________
3. ____________________

WEEK 2: ____________________

FINANCIAL GOAL
1. ____________________
2. ____________________
3. ____________________

Paycheck Budget #2

USE THIS SECTION TO KEEP TRACK OF MONTHLY EXPENSES.
IF YOU HAVE MORE BILLS THAN THE SPACE LISTED, REEVALUATE WHAT'S IMPORTANT.

MONTH OF: ____________________

NEXT PAYCHECK: ____________________

PAYCHECK #1 GROSS INCOME: ____________________

TAXES/DEDUCTIONS TAKEN OUT: ____________________

PAYCHECK #1 NET INCOME: ____________________

ANY FINANCIAL EMERGENCIES HAPPEN THIS MONTH? LIST THEM BELOW.

PAYEE	AMOUNT	DATE	BALANCE

BILL TOTAL: ____________________

Bi-Weekly Financial To Do List

USE THIS SECTION TO LIST ANY TASKS OR ERRANDS NEEDED FOR THE WEEK.
FOR EXAMPLE, MAKING A BANK WITHDRAWAL OR DEPOSITING MONEY IN SAVINGS.

WEEK 3: ____________________

FINANCIAL GOAL
1. ______________________________
2. ______________________________
3. ______________________________

WEEK 4: ____________________

FINANCIAL GOAL
1. ______________________________
2. ______________________________
3. ______________________________

My Monthly Savings Plan

USE THIS SECTION TO LIST YOUR SAVINGS GOAL
AND MONTHLY CONTRIBUTIONS

IF AN UNEXPECTED EMERGENCY HAPPENED, HOW MUCH WOULD I NEED TO SURVIVE FOR 6 MONTHS?

$____________________

ONE YEAR? $____________________

HOW MUCH SAVINGS WOULD MAKE ME FEEL "SAFE"? $____________________

CURRENT MONTHLY SAVINGS CONTRIBUTION $____________________

CUSHION SAVINGS GOAL? $____________________

SEPARATE RETIREMENT ACCOUNTS (MONTHLY) $____________________

CAN I INCREASE MY CONTRIBUTION THIS MONTH? $____________________

IF YES, BY HOW MUCH? $____________________

RETIREMENT (WORK-RELATED)? $____________________

IRA ROTH? $____________________

IRA TRADITIONAL? $____________________

ANY UNEXPECTED MONEY THIS MONTH?

IF YES, HOW WILL I USE IT? ______________________________

____

____

My Monthly Debt Payoff

USE THIS SECTION TO LIST ALL YOUR DEBTS YOU ARE CURRENTLY PAYING ON EACH MONTH

PAYEE	CURRENT BALANCE	AMOUNT PAID	ENDING BALANCE	DATE

Y O U G O T T H I S

TOTAL DEBT BEFORE PAYMENTS: $ ______________________

TOTAL AMOUNT AFTER PAYMENTS $ ______________________

Monthly Notes

3rd Quarter Check-In

My Financial Check-in

USE THIS SECTION TO TAKE ACCOUNTABILITY AND BE HONEST WITH YOUR JOURNEY OVER THE PAST THREE MONTHS.

REVIEW

HOW'S IT GOING SO FAR? ANY SETBACKS? ANY MILESTONES?

ADJUST

WHAT CAN I DO TO ADJUST THIS SETBACK? HOW WILL I CELEBRATE THIS MILESTONE?

Short Notes

Financial Check-in Continued...

EXECUTE

HOW WILL I IMPLEMENT THIS NEW ADJUSTMENT INTO MY FINANCIAL PLAN?

MONITOR

WHAT DOES MY FINANCIAL MONITORING ROUTINE LOOK LIKE? IS IT WORKING?

Short Notes

Credit Score Check-In

HAVE YOU CHECKED YOUR CREDIT?

AVAILABLE ONLINE RESOURCES:

CREDIT KARMA
WWW.CREDITKARMA.COM

CREDIT SESAME
WWW.CREDITSESAME.COM

EXPERIAN
WWW.EXPERIAN.COM

EQUIFAX
WWW.EQUIFAX.COM

TRANSUNION
WWW.TRANSUNION.COM

MY FICO SCORE
WWW.MYFICO.COM

EXPERIAN SCORE

EQUIFAX SCORE

Short Notes

TRANSUNIION SCORE

LIST YOUR GOAL SCORE HERE:

WHAT ARE SOME THINGS I CAN DO TO INCREASE MY CREDIT IN THE NEXT QUARTER?

Month 10

Monthly Expense Tracker

USE THIS SECTION TO KEEP TRACK OF MONTHLY EXPENSES OUTSIDE OF YOUR BUDGET. WAS THE ITEM A NEED OR A WANT?

ITEM DESCRIPTION	AMOUNT SPENT	NEED / WANT?

TOTAL: ______________________

Paycheck Budget #1

USE THIS SECTION TO KEEP TRACK OF MONTHLY EXPENSES.
IF YOU HAVE MORE BILLS THAN THE SPACE LISTED, REEVALUATE WHAT'S IMPORTANT.

MONTH OF: ______________________

PAYCHECK #1 GROSS INCOME: ____________________

NEXT PAYCHECK: ______________

TAXES/DEDUCTIONS TAKEN OUT: __________________

PAYCHECK #1 NET INCOME: ______________________

ANY FINANCIAL EMERGENCIES
HAPPEN THIS MONTH?
LIST THEM BELOW.

PAYEE	AMOUNT	DATE	BALANCE

BILL TOTAL: ______________

Bi-Weekly Financial To Do List

USE THIS SECTION TO LIST ANY TASKS OR ERRANDS NEEDED FOR THE WEEK.
FOR EXAMPLE, MAKING A BANK WITHDRAWAL OR DEPOSITING MONEY IN SAVINGS.

WEEK 1: ______________

FINANCIAL GOAL
1. ______________
2. ______________
3. ______________

WEEK 2: ______________

FINANCIAL GOAL
1. ______________
2. ______________
3. ______________

Paycheck Budget #2

USE THIS SECTION TO KEEP TRACK OF MONTHLY EXPENSES.
IF YOU HAVE MORE BILLS THAN THE SPACE LISTED, REEVALUATE WHAT'S IMPORTANT.

MONTH OF: ____________________

NEXT PAYCHECK: ______________

PAYCHECK #1 GROSS INCOME: ____________________

TAXES/DEDUCTIONS TAKEN OUT: ________________

PAYCHECK #1 NET INCOME: ____________________

ANY FINANCIAL EMERGENCIES
HAPPEN THIS MONTH?
LIST THEM BELOW.

PAYEE	AMOUNT	DATE	BALANCE

BILL TOTAL: ______________

Bi-Weekly Financial To Do List

USE THIS SECTION TO LIST ANY TASKS OR ERRANDS NEEDED FOR THE WEEK.
FOR EXAMPLE, MAKING A BANK WITHDRAWAL OR DEPOSITING MONEY IN SAVINGS.

WEEK 3: ________________

FINANCIAL GOAL
1. ______________________________
2. ______________________________
3. ______________________________

WEEK 4: ________________

FINANCIAL GOAL
1. ______________________________
2. ______________________________
3. ______________________________

My Monthly Savings Plan

USE THIS SECTION TO LIST YOUR SAVINGS GOAL
AND MONTHLY CONTRIBUTIONS

IF AN UNEXPECTED EMERGENCY HAPPENED, HOW MUCH WOULD I NEED TO SURVIVE FOR 6 MONTHS?

$________________

ONE YEAR? $________________

HOW MUCH SAVINGS WOULD MAKE ME FEEL "SAFE"? $________________

CURRENT MONTHLY SAVINGS CONTRIBUTION $________________

CUSHION SAVINGS GOAL? $________________

SEPARATE RETIREMENT ACCOUNTS (MONTHLY) $________________

CAN I INCREASE MY CONTRIBUTION THIS MONTH? $________________

IF YES, BY HOW MUCH? $________________

RETIREMENT (WORK-RELATED)? $________________

IRA ROTH? $________________

IRA TRADITIONAL? $________________

ANY UNEXPECTED MONEY THIS MONTH?

IF YES, HOW WILL I USE IT? ________________

____

____

My Monthly Debt Payoff

USE THIS SECTION TO LIST ALL YOUR DEBTS YOU ARE CURRENTLY PAYING ON EACH MONTH

PAYEE	CURRENT BALANCE	AMOUNT PAID	ENDING BALANCE	DATE

TOTAL DEBT BEFORE PAYMENTS: $ ____________________

TOTAL AMOUNT AFTER PAYMENTS $ ____________________

YOU GOT THIS

Monthly Notes

Month 11

Monthly Expense Tracker

USE THIS SECTION TO KEEP TRACK OF MONTHLY EXPENSES
OUTSIDE OF YOUR BUDGET. WAS THE ITEM A NEED OR A WANT?

ITEM DESCRIPTION	AMOUNT SPENT	NEED / WANT?

TOTAL: ______________________

Paycheck Budget #1

USE THIS SECTION TO KEEP TRACK OF MONTHLY EXPENSES.
IF YOU HAVE MORE BILLS THAN THE SPACE LISTED, REEVALUATE WHAT'S IMPORTANT.

MONTH OF: ____________________

PAYCHECK #1 GROSS INCOME: ____________________

NEXT PAYCHECK: ______________

TAXES/DEDUCTIONS TAKEN OUT: ____________________

PAYCHECK #1 NET INCOME: ____________________

ANY FINANCIAL EMERGENCIES
HAPPEN THIS MONTH?
LIST THEM BELOW.

PAYEE	AMOUNT	DATE	BALANCE

BILL TOTAL: ______________

Bi-Weekly Financial To Do List

USE THIS SECTION TO LIST ANY TASKS OR ERRANDS NEEDED FOR THE WEEK.
FOR EXAMPLE, MAKING A BANK WITHDRAWAL OR DEPOSITING MONEY IN SAVINGS.

WEEK 1: ____________________

FINANCIAL GOAL
1. ____________________
2. ____________________
3. ____________________

WEEK 2: ____________________

FINANCIAL GOAL
1. ____________________
2. ____________________
3. ____________________

Paycheck Budget #2

USE THIS SECTION TO KEEP TRACK OF MONTHLY EXPENSES.
IF YOU HAVE MORE BILLS THAN THE SPACE LISTED, REEVALUATE WHAT'S IMPORTANT.

MONTH OF: ______________________

NEXT PAYCHECK: ______________

PAYCHECK #1 GROSS INCOME: ______________________

TAXES/DEDUCTIONS TAKEN OUT: ____________________

PAYCHECK #1 NET INCOME: ________________________

PAYEE	AMOUNT	DATE	BALANCE

ANY FINANCIAL EMERGENCIES HAPPEN THIS MONTH? LIST THEM BELOW.

____
____
____
____

____
____
____
____

BILL TOTAL: ______________

Bi-Weekly Financial To Do List

USE THIS SECTION TO LIST ANY TASKS OR ERRANDS NEEDED FOR THE WEEK.
FOR EXAMPLE, MAKING A BANK WITHDRAWAL OR DEPOSITING MONEY IN SAVINGS.

WEEK 3: ________________

FINANCIAL GOAL
1. ________________________________
2. ________________________________
3. ________________________________

WEEK 4: ________________

FINANCIAL GOAL
1. ________________________________
2. ________________________________
3. ________________________________

My Monthly Savings Plan

USE THIS SECTION TO LIST YOUR SAVINGS GOAL
AND MONTHLY CONTRIBUTIONS

IF AN UNEXPECTED EMERGENCY HAPPENED, HOW MUCH WOULD I NEED TO SURVIVE FOR 6 MONTHS?

$____________________

ONE YEAR? $____________________

HOW MUCH SAVINGS WOULD MAKE ME FEEL "SAFE"? $____________________

CURRENT MONTHLY SAVINGS CONTRIBUTION $____________________

CUSHION SAVINGS GOAL? $____________________

SEPARATE RETIREMENT ACCOUNTS (MONTHLY) $____________________

CAN I INCREASE MY CONTRIBUTION THIS MONTH? $____________________

IF YES, BY HOW MUCH? $____________________

RETIREMENT (WORK-RELATED)? $____________________

IRA ROTH? $____________________

IRA TRADITIONAL? $____________________

ANY UNEXPECTED MONEY THIS MONTH?

IF YES, HOW WILL I USE IT? ____________________________________

____

____

My Monthly Debt Payoff

USE THIS SECTION TO LIST ALL YOUR DEBTS YOU ARE CURRENTLY PAYING ON EACH MONTH

PAYEE	CURRENT BALANCE	AMOUNT PAID	ENDING BALANCE	DATE

Y O U G O T T H I S

TOTAL DEBT BEFORE PAYMENTS: $ ______________________

TOTAL AMOUNT AFTER PAYMENTS $ ______________________

Monthly Notes

Month 12

Monthly Expense Tracker

USE THIS SECTION TO KEEP TRACK OF MONTHLY EXPENSES OUTSIDE OF YOUR BUDGET. WAS THE ITEM A NEED OR A WANT?

ITEM DESCRIPTION	AMOUNT SPENT	NEED / WANT?

TOTAL: ____________________

Paycheck Budget #1

USE THIS SECTION TO KEEP TRACK OF MONTHLY EXPENSES.
IF YOU HAVE MORE BILLS THAN THE SPACE LISTED, REEVALUATE WHAT'S IMPORTANT.

MONTH OF: ____________________

PAYCHECK #1 GROSS INCOME: ____________________

NEXT PAYCHECK: ______________

TAXES/DEDUCTIONS TAKEN OUT: ________________

PAYCHECK #1 NET INCOME: ____________________

ANY FINANCIAL EMERGENCIES HAPPEN THIS MONTH? LIST THEM BELOW.

PAYEE	AMOUNT	DATE	BALANCE

____

____

____

____

____

____

____

____

BILL TOTAL: ______________

Bi-Weekly Financial To Do List

USE THIS SECTION TO LIST ANY TASKS OR ERRANDS NEEDED FOR THE WEEK.
FOR EXAMPLE, MAKING A BANK WITHDRAWAL OR DEPOSITING MONEY IN SAVINGS.

WEEK 1: ________________

FINANCIAL GOAL
1. ________________
2. ________________
3. ________________

WEEK 2: ________________

FINANCIAL GOAL
1. ________________
2. ________________
3. ________________

Paycheck Budget #2

USE THIS SECTION TO KEEP TRACK OF MONTHLY EXPENSES.
IF YOU HAVE MORE BILLS THAN THE SPACE LISTED, REEVALUATE WHAT'S IMPORTANT.

MONTH OF: ____________________

PAYCHECK #1 GROSS INCOME: ____________________

NEXT PAYCHECK: ____________________

TAXES/DEDUCTIONS TAKEN OUT: ____________________

PAYCHECK #1 NET INCOME: ____________________

ANY FINANCIAL EMERGENCIES
HAPPEN THIS MONTH?
LIST THEM BELOW.

PAYEE	AMOUNT	DATE	BALANCE

BILL TOTAL: ____________________

Bi-Weekly Financial To Do List

USE THIS SECTION TO LIST ANY TASKS OR ERRANDS NEEDED FOR THE WEEK.
FOR EXAMPLE, MAKING A BANK WITHDRAWAL OR DEPOSITING MONEY IN SAVINGS.

WEEK 3: ______________

FINANCIAL GOAL
1. ______________
2. ______________
3. ______________

WEEK 4: ______________

FINANCIAL GOAL
1. ______________
2. ______________
3. ______________

My Monthly Savings Plan

USE THIS SECTION TO LIST YOUR SAVINGS GOAL
AND MONTHLY CONTRIBUTIONS

IF AN UNEXPECTED EMERGENCY HAPPENED, HOW MUCH WOULD I NEED TO SURVIVE FOR 6 MONTHS?

$______________________

ONE YEAR? $______________________

HOW MUCH SAVINGS WOULD MAKE ME FEEL "SAFE"? $______________________

CURRENT MONTHLY SAVINGS CONTRIBUTION $______________________

CUSHION SAVINGS GOAL? $______________________

SEPARATE RETIREMENT ACCOUNTS (MONTHLY) $______________________

CAN I INCREASE MY CONTRIBUTION THIS MONTH? $______________________

IF YES, BY HOW MUCH? $______________________

RETIREMENT (WORK-RELATED)? $______________________

IRA ROTH? $______________________

IRA TRADITIONAL? $______________________

ANY UNEXPECTED MONEY THIS MONTH?

IF YES, HOW WILL I USE IT? ______________________

____

____

My Monthly Debt Payoff

USE THIS SECTION TO LIST ALL YOUR DEBTS YOU ARE CURRENTLY PAYING ON EACH MONTH

PAYEE	CURRENT BALANCE	AMOUNT PAID	ENDING BALANCE	DATE

Y O U G O T T H I S

TOTAL DEBT BEFORE PAYMENTS: $ ____________________

TOTAL AMOUNT AFTER PAYMENTS $ ____________________

Monthly Notes

4th Quarter Check-In

Financial Check-in Continued...

EXECUTE

HOW WILL I IMPLEMENT THIS NEW ADJUSTMENT INTO MY FINANCIAL PLAN?

MONITOR

WHAT DOES MY FINANCIAL MONITORING ROUTINE LOOK LIKE? IS IT WORKING?

Short Notes

My Financial Check-in

USE THIS SECTION TO TAKE ACCOUNTABILITY AND BE HONEST WITH YOUR JOURNEY OVER THE PAST THREE MONTHS.

REVIEW

HOW'S IT GOING SO FAR? ANY SETBACKS? ANY MILESTONES?

ADJUST

WHAT CAN I DO TO ADJUST THIS SETBACK? HOW WILL I CELEBRATE THIS MILESTONE?

Short Notes

Credit Score Check-In

HAVE YOU CHECKED YOUR CREDIT?

AVAILABLE ONLINE RESOURCES:

CREDIT KARMA
WWW.CREDITKARMA.COM

CREDIT SESAME
WWW.CREDITSESAME.COM

EXPERIAN
WWW.EXPERIAN.COM

EQUIFAX
WWW.EQUIFAX.COM

TRANSUNION
WWW.TRANSUNION.COM

MY FICO SCORE
WWW.MYFICO.COM

EXPERIAN SCORE

EQUIFAX SCORE

Short Notes

TRANSUNIION SCORE

LIST YOUR GOAL SCORE HERE:

WHAT ARE SOME THINGS I CAN DO TO INCREASE MY CREDIT IN THE NEXT QUARTER?

Made in the USA
Monee, IL
02 November 2026

67376992R00083